Foreword

> *"Coaching doesn't make sick people well...*
> *it helps healthy people become extra-ordinary"*
> — *Thomas J. Leonard, founder of Coach University*

Life Habits for Leaders was originally intended to be a large coaching manual. After many edits and numerous discussions with my editor, it was scaled down to its current size.

Coaching was a relatively new term and profession when I entered it in 1994. I enrolled in one of the first coaching schools, Coach University (AKA CoachU), and quickly learned through my clients that people will do what they want to do despite what they say. This was a huge lesson to learn, and one that I keep relearning.

The other big reality that hits you square in the face as you begin coaching is: you can't coach someone who does not want to be coached.

I think you will agree that coaching is not for everyone… but leadership most certainly is. And judging by today's headlines, good leadership is sorely needed.

Consider this short book a handbook on the art of leadership. It is by no means complete, but it addresses many of the essential components of leadership that we all need to embrace, and we all need to be occasionally reminded of.

Lead well.

Jeff Pasquale
Boynton Beach, Florida
March 16, 2014

inspiring
AUTHENTICITY acknowledge   TRUST
steady nonjudgmental positive   truthful   assists gossip-free trustworthy
growth   enthusiastic   EMPOWER   recognize integrity
CONSISTENCY fairness power shared-authority   ethical
predictable understandable real open purposeful guide   harmony
responsive dependable connection confidence delegate inspired purposeful praise
focus persistent approachable happy   constructive

Changing the World

LIFE HABITS
FOR LEADERS

Right Where You Are

caring   action considerate   giving
encourage   SIMPLICITY   energized   CREATIVITY
COURAGE confident steady clutter peaceful balanced passionate help without-boundaries
appreciate patience organized uncomplicated goals even-tempered privilege artistic
legacy unafraid easy concise aware accountability care imagine create serves
clarity decisive focused CHANGE excited opportunity
vision   fun

Jeff Pasquale

ISBN: 978-0-9896603-4-1

Editor: Kammy Wood and Christy Distler
Text layout and design: Lorie DeWorken, Mind*the*Margins
Cover design: Lorie DeWorken, Mind*the*Margins

More information about Jeff can be found at www.JeffPasquale.com

For Stephen R. Covey and Thomas J. Leonard

Contents

Introduction

"...the person who scored well on an SAT will not necessarily be the best doctor or the best lawyer or the best businessman. These tests do not measure character, leadership, creativity, perseverance."
– William Julius Wilson

Although I am an acknowledged optimist, I have to say that by all appearances, our society is really screwed up.

How we got to this point of economic and moral disarray in the second decade of the twenty-first century will be argued for years to come. But for now, the most important question we can ask ourselves is, *"What am I going to do about it?"* The "it" in question is the unreliability and unpredictability of the world around us—our people and our institutions.

Much of this disarray can be attributed to a lack of trusted leadership in this country and around the world. Because of this leadership void, we are also directionless. It seems that all our leaders can accomplish is making sure that they get "theirs" first.

We all need to play a role in changing this *me-first* mentality.

We need to clear up our misunderstanding about what a leader is and who a leader should be.

THE LOST ART OF LEADERSHIP

Today, we don't need more information to succeed. We need perspective. We all know about the importance of playing by the rules, and the importance of being fair and ethical. But knowing we need to be ethical is not enough. We need to consistently put these ideals into action and we need to see them working successfully.

We learn by example, and we look to our leaders for examples in action. Leadership, when it is intentional, can have a tremendously powerful and positive effect on others—in business, in life, and around the world.

Genuine leadership, by many accounts, is a dying art. We see executives being carted off to prison for stealing, or we hear they've been dismissed for inappropriate behavior with a fellow employee. Then a few months later, they're spotlighted in the media promoting their new books and speaking tours, sharing their downfalls and profiting from them.

The unfortunate reality is that we accept this as business as usual. We are no longer surprised or shocked by this type of behavior. Yet we still want to be inspired by our leaders. We

Changing the world

want obvious reminders that our work has meaning. These reminders must come from both our leaders' behaviors and actions and from our own beliefs and actions.

We need an improved set of habits for leaders to embrace. As Stephen Covey, author of *The 7 Habits of Highly Effective People*, offered: "If you're going to make the effort to climb the ladder of success, make sure the ladder is up against the right wall."

EVERYONE IS A LEADER

There may be a handful of born leaders in the world. (That is, really great leaders.) The rest of us must learn continuously, through trial and error, and with intention.

Most people avoid the deliberate decision to be a leader— probably because it's easier to say, "It's not my job" than it is to take responsibility. But sometimes it's because of fear. Fear of making the wrong decision. Fear of being disliked.

People also avoid being a leader because they believe that unless they're in charge, they're not leading. Not true at all.

Each one of us is a leader. Whether we fill the role of parent, neighbor, friend, church member, community member, employee, volunteer, partner, pedestrian, runner, or bicyclist, every day we have an opportunity, sometimes even an obligation, to lead.

Consider the roles you play in your personal life right now. In virtually all of them, you are a leader to someone. You are a leader by your actions, by your behaviors, and by your attitudes, all of which are visible to those around you—whether or not you are aware of it. For example, if you think for one moment that a simple lie that is offered in the presence of your children (who know it's a lie) does not impact them, you're kidding yourself.

The same is true for your role at work. Habits such as taking shortcuts, spreading rumors, or knocking a company decision will affect those around you.

Leadership is about being aware that people are watching and taking note of what we do, positively or negatively, whether or not we notice they're watching.

Seek to make a difference now and to start acting like the leader that you are. Set and adhere to higher personal standards. Pay attention to what you do.

A NEW WAY OF LEADING (THAT ISN'T NEW AT ALL)

You can improve your own leadership capabilities by simply asking yourself these three questions every day:

> *Am I being **authentic** with myself and with others?*

> *Am I living and communicating as **simply** as I possibly can?*

> *Am I **consistent** in everything I think, do, and say?*

A universal truth about the Life Habits is, if you model great life (leadership) habits, others will learn from you, whether they intend to or not.

Everyone is a leader to someone, and it is every leader's responsibility to rise above the temptation to take the easy way out. Leadership is not about taking something that isn't yours or holding someone back because you fear they will get more than you.

While it's easy to push leadership responsibility onto others, it's not so easy to dispel the effect we have on those around us, whether we do something grand or we shirk our leadership responsibilities.

We are all impressionable. If we weren't, advertisers wouldn't spend millions of dollars trying to influence our buying decisions with magazines, billboards, the Internet, and television ads.

OUR ACTIONS

The new reality is that one silly line from a television commercial or a YouTube video can get the attention of millions of people. Imagine the effect you can have on people who see or hear about something good (or bad) that you've done. People *are* paying attention to what we do.

A perfect example is holding the door open for someone. Let's say you are walking through the doorway of a building; instead of letting the door close behind you, you stand for an extra five or ten seconds and hold the door for the next person. While it's a simple gesture of kindness, it also helps the person behind you feel valued.

Anyone who witnessed the extra time you spent helping someone else registered this event, consciously or unconsciously.

Imagine the contrasting scenario. This time it's raining and the person behind you has both hands full, but you walk in and let the door shut behind you. A bystander may assume you're a jackass. Or he or she may assume you're busy, distracted, or just inconsiderate. In that brief moment, people *do* make decisions about the actions of people they do not know.

THE CULTURE OF A COMPANY

The culture of a company is similar. Have you ever walked through an office of a company whose employees are smiling and upbeat? They make eye contact and even hellos are exchanged. You can feel the positive energy.

You have also probably been in an office where you can feel the tension. There, the people are somber, tired, and distracted—you don't see smiles.

The leaders of these companies have either allowed these cultures to form or they have modeled this behavior themselves...or both. The people who work for these leaders tend to embody their styles and philosophies.

The simple act of helping a stranger, smiling, or saying thank you are all examples of leading. You constantly influence others without even knowing it.

We are all leaders.

With so much attention placed on leadership over the years, the art and practice of skillful management seems to have taken a back seat. The Life Habits will complement and enhance your management skills.

The Life Habits can be especially effective at work, but they will also apply to your personal life.

The self-assessments within each chapter were designed to raise your awareness level about the subtle and unique aspects of leadership; they were not meant to point out your deficiencies or your perceived failings.

When taking the self-assessments, do your best to avoid judging yourself. (Sometimes you just can't help it.) But the more you become aware of your tendency to judge yourself, the more clearly you will understand the intent behind each of the self-assessments in this book.

And don't let the self-assessments control you either. They are perspectives, ideals, and things we strive for. They are indicators of where you are at this moment; it doesn't mean that this is who you are all the time. So rather than beating yourself up over it, acknowledge where you would like to improve, intend to do better, and get on with your day.

When you know where you stand and exactly what you want, the more capabilities and opportunities you'll have to change and improve things.

inspiring
AUTHENTICITY
nonjudgmental   positive
enthusiastic
power
real
connection
approachable
happy
open

LIFE HABIT ONE
Be Authentic

*"If you tell the truth,
you don't have to remember anything."*

– Mark Twain

While the concept of authenticity might be a bit overused, it genuinely needs to be covered here. A person is either real or he isn't. (Real as in authentic or "not phony.")

Authenticity is vital to every successful relationship. Marriage partners need it, business partners need it, companies need it, schools need it, and families need it.

Being authentic means being your true self—you know who you are, you are clear about what's important to you, and you consistently honor what you value by walking your talk. Authenticity is not a technique; it's who you are (or who you intend to become). As a leader, it is better to model authenticity for your employees than to preach it.

Remember the advice you received as you went for your first job interview? *Just be yourself.*

Solid counsel. No hype. Just simple advice straight from the heart.

Authenticity is no different; it exists when there is a direct connection between our values and our thoughts, words, and deeds. Authenticity is neither right nor wrong; it is a reflection of who you really are.

A person who is authentic is open to the world, is easily approachable, is someone who readily honors his or her values and is naturally complete or whole. Whether you want to improve yourself (or your company), it all starts with you.

It is powerful as well as inspiring for a person to respond in the same manner regardless of the situation he is facing. In other words, he is the same person with his spouse as he is in front of three hundred employees. He doesn't pretend, and everyone in his presence is aware of it.

Authenticity is power, but not the kind of power to impress or trick others. You don't seek praise for being authentic and you make no apologies for your faults. You are happy with who you are.

Typically, an authentic person is happy; she rarely, if ever, appears moody or angry. The authentic individual tends to have a very upbeat, enthusiastic, and positive viewpoint of herself and the world around her. She tends to attract like-minded individuals into her life, as well as to the business she's building.

To be authentic is to allow yourself to be vulnerable; to risk criticism, judgment, or dismissal. As leaders we should embrace our missteps as openly as our achievements. Authenticity requires no less.

AUTHENTICITY

Recognizing authenticity is sometimes intuitive; you can't always prove when someone is not being authentic, but you can definitely feel it.

The following self-assessment is a guide to help you gauge the level of authenticity in your life.

INSTRUCTIONS: Read each statement. If the statement is true for you, check it.

____ When I communicate with others, I say what I mean and mean what I say.

____ My actions support the commitments I make.

____ I recognize when something is bothering me, but I don't let it interfere with what I'm trying to accomplish.

____ I am known as a person who keeps his/her word.

____ I am basically the same person whether I am with my boss, my peers, my employees, my family, or my friends.

____ People have an easy time understanding who I am and where I'm coming from when they interact with me.

_____ I am comfortable with who I am and where I am going with my life.

_____ If people who know me were asked about my personality, they would definitely say that I am a "real" person.

_____ TOTAL

AUTHENTICITY

IS	IS NOT
Keeping your word	Overpromising
Apologizing	Making excuses
Dealing with issues	Avoiding issues
Being decisive	Acting evasively
Being naturally happy	Forcing a smile
Being glad to see people	Tolerating others
Being totally present	Continuously multi-tasking
Having an inclusive attitude	Excluding others
Expressing frustration	Hiding your feelings

ACTIONS

1. Whenever you catch yourself saying things that you know are not accurate, take a moment to think things through. Don't make excuses to yourself. If you are not being authentic, acknowledge it and then correct it.

2. Notice whenever you feel pressured or uneasy about things and how often it happens. See if you can determine the cause of those feelings.

3. Hold yourself to a higher standard. You're not going to impose your standards on others—but if you lead by example, and one of those examples is having high standards, those around you will tend to respond in kind.

4. Acknowledge when you sense other people are not being authentic. Don't judge them or call them on it, just notice it— how it feels, what it sounds like and looks like. Acknowledge that you sound and look the same way to others when you choose not to be authentic yourself.

SIMPLICITY
free
steady
Clutter
organized
peaceful balanced
uncomplicated
easy concise

LIFE HABIT TWO
Embrace Simplicity

"Simplicity, simplicity, simplicity!
I say, let your affairs be as two or three,
and not a hundred or a thousand;
instead of a million count half a dozen,
and keep your accounts on your thumb nail."
– Henry David Thoreau

The second Life Habit is sometimes a little tricky because it sounds so easy. But simplicity can be one of the most difficult things to attain as a leader. You cannot instill simplicity into your company until simplicity is instilled in your life.

Life has become too complex. We make it that way, even if we're not willing to admit it. Sometimes we fall into the trap of believing that life has to be complicated. It doesn't.

Life can be simple.

Simplicity is a basic need, if not a requirement, for most people today, yet we feel it is impossible to achieve. Or we don't recognize its importance. After all, our world is crammed with PIN numbers, user IDs, and passwords.

When we do remember these codes, it's to gain access to our voicemail, email, bank accounts, cars, and home alarm systems, which then requires us to know how to *operate* those systems. We have to know how to program our watches, DVD players, or microwaves, and each differs from brand to brand.

While this is certainly no crisis, the fact remains that too many aspects of our personal and professional lives are overly complicated.

A complicated lifestyle drains us of energy. Likewise, when we are in the company of people who live a complicated lifestyle, they drain our energy, too.

Because it's easy to find fault with others, the best step you can take as a leader is to take care of your own life first. It's hard to promote simplicity if you have junk piled up all around you.

If your schedule is so hectic that you find yourself struggling just to get simple things accomplished in your personal life (doctor appointments, haircuts, family outings), then the universe is trying to tell you something. To achieve balance in your life, you must *intend* for simplicity to occur. Likewise, a leader must intend for simplicity to occur. You can't expect someone else to create it for you.

You cannot simplify your life in a day, week, or month. It will take months. But you can simplify things one plan, appointment, or commitment at a time. Give yourself the time and the space for simplicity to take root.

SIMPLICITY

Simplicity is a way of life and a standard by which to lead your life, which improves your effectiveness and lessens your struggles.

The following self-assessment is a guide to help you gauge the level of simplicity in your life.

INSTRUCTIONS: Read each statement. If the statement is true for you, check it.

____ I keep my work area organized and unobstructed.

____ I have my files organized in such a way that it's easy to put my hands on whatever I'm looking for.

____ I have a minimum of clutter in my life; that includes possessions, commitments, and thoughts.

____ I speak and write in such a way that nearly everyone I come in contact with understands me.

____ I rarely find myself confused or overwhelmed by circumstances at home or at work.

____ I try to speak in concise (as in short, to-the-point) messages, rather than lengthy explanations.

____ I break problems, concerns, and strategies down into chunks so that they are easier for me (and for others) to understand and act upon.

____ I am part of an organization that values simplicity; I believe in making it easy for clients to do business with us.

____ TOTAL

SIMPLICITY

<u>IS</u>	<u>IS NOT</u>
Using plain language	Using doubletalk
Getting back to basics	Intricate detail
Achieving steady growth	Erratic performance
Having a calming presence	Being a stress inducer
Telling a story	Reciting facts and statistics
Listening before speaking	Talking before listening
Easy to be with	Never at peace
Having a short to-do list	A planner full of Post-It notes

ACTIONS

1. The next time you have written something—a letter, email, etc.—revise it. No matter how long it is, reduce it to half of its original size. Aggressively practice this.

2. Stop over-explaining things. Catch yourself when you are talking too much in any setting—personal or business. Begin saying less immediately. See how it feels; notice the reactions of the people who are with you.

steady
growth
CONSISTENCY fairness
predictable   understandable
responsive   dependable
persistent

LIFE HABIT THREE
Practice Consistency

"Consistency is the foundation of virtue."
– Francis Bacon

Consistency is a crucial habit, yet we hardly seem to take much notice of it. It can be the most difficult Life Habit to embrace, but it is also extremely powerful.

Consistency is not mystical or magical. Consistency as a leader means you are dependable and predictable in word, thought, and deed.

It doesn't matter what your position is in an organization— if you are inconsistent, it eventually affects everyone around you. You owe it to all your personal and professional relationships to provide steady, consistent leadership.

Perhaps the biggest personal impact you can have as a leader when dealing with other people is to practice fairness. When others recognize that they can expect a consistently fair response from you as their leader, respect, goodwill, and innovation increase exponentially because fear is absent from the equation.

When you strive to consistently be yourself in every situation you face, and the people around you gain a comfort level, they will tend to become more like you in demeanor and action.

Consistency is exemplified by how you conduct yourself or how you respond to things, especially when you take the time to listen to employees or customers.

Consistency builds relationships. Each party in a relationship trusts the other person's responses and reactions based on the history of their relationship.

If you willingly help your child one day because he asked, and the next day you yell at him for asking again, he would stop asking for help. The same holds true with inconsistent leadership. Is that the reaction you want?

CONSISTENCY
Consistency is being who you really are on a daily basis.

The following self-assessment is a guide to help you gauge the level of consistency in your life.

INSTRUCTIONS: Read each statement. If the statement is true for you, check it.

____ I am able to stay focused on my plans and my goals; I don't jump from one thing to another and leave things incomplete.

____ I have fair expectations for myself and others when it comes to my relationships. I believe it's a two-way street.

____ I am consistent in a good way—I am predicable, but I'm not a robot.

____ I'm innovative; nearly everything I touch or that am working on is moving forward on a steady basis.

____ My values and standards are easily understood by others because of my consistent attitude and behaviors.

____ I consistently view myself as the catalyst that keeps my world growing and moving forward.

____ I consistently strive to be myself at all times—not playing a role that I think I should be.

____ I am predictable in the sense that both strangers and friends can easily determine where I stand on things that I consider important.

____ TOTAL

CONSISTENCY

<u>IS</u>	<u>IS NOT</u>
Predictability	Creating unpleasant surprises
Congruent behavior (few extremes)	Saying one thing/doing another
Providing honest input/ feedback	Dancing around the subject
Telling the truth	Sugarcoating everything
Steady leadership	Constantly changing your mind/direction
Recurring themes/messages	Mixed or changing messages
Behaving the same way with one person or fifty people	Constantly changing personalities
Possessing empowering habits	Being an Activity-of-the-Month participant

ACTIONS

1. Over the past five years, what three standards or values do you believe you have consistently stood for?

2. How about for the past ten years?

3. How about the last twenty years?

4. What are the top three values or standards you would most like to be known for?

5. What areas of your life (both personally and profession-ally) do you feel you are consistently most effective in?

LIFE HABIT FOUR
Give and Receive Trust

assists *gossip-free* *commitment* **TRUST** *trustworthy* *praise* *integrity* *ethical* *harmony* *purposeful* *constructive*

"You can't talk your way out of a situation that you've behaved yourself into."
– Stephen Covey

Trust is sometimes hard to define. You can't measure it, you can't see it, and you can't feel it…but you will notice when it's not there.

As a leader, in order to have trust in your personal or professional relationships, you need to be trustworthy. The reality is that untrustworthy people are always in our midst. While it is important to be able to identify those who are not trustworthy, it is more important to focus on those who are.

I'm not suggesting that you turn a blind eye to dishonest people, but there is another way to increase the number of trustworthy people that you work and associate with: being trustworthy yourself is the most reliable means of attracting like people.

Trust begins with you as a leader, which means you have to set the example. To successfully embrace the Life Habit of trust, you must model the type of trustworthiness you want to see in your company and in the people you lead. When you are clear about how you want to model and embrace trustworthiness, you will quickly begin to spot those same positive behaviors in others.

When you look for the good in people, you naturally become a more trusting person.

The primary trait we all instinctively look for in a leader is trustworthiness. Will this person make a promise to me and not keep it? Change the rules or the requirements and not tell me? Talk behind my back? Or say one thing to me and something different to another person?

As you practice the habit of trust, you will find that it has more to do with your actions than your words. But when you use words, they had better match your actions!

GIVE AND RECEIVE TRUST

Trust is an extremely difficult thing to earn and keep, especially when a leader is knee-deep in his or her own challenges. Trust is something a leader has to give first before receiving it.

The following self-assessment is a guide to help you gauge the level of trust in your life.

INSTRUCTIONS: Read each statement. If the statement is true for you, check it.

____ I never give others reason to doubt my integrity or my ethics.

____ My actions are in full harmony with my words.

____ I follow through on and meet all the commitments I make.

____ I use a planner or a planning device to schedule the things that are important to me—personally and professionally.

____ I look people in the eye when I speak with them.

____ I recognize people for their efforts.

____ I provide constructive criticism in a private environment and I expect the same from those I lead.

____ If I don't know something, I say, "I don't know."

____ TOTAL

TRUST

<u>IS</u>	<u>IS NOT</u>
Taking time to listen	Rolling eyes in exasperation
Being upbeat and positive	Being crabby and threatening
Offering advice	Pointing out nitpicky mistakes
Complimenting effort	Belittling employees
Constructive criticism in private	Admonishing in public
Providing realistic feedback	Sarcasm
Praising those not present	Bad-mouthing those not present
Offering help or assistance	Placing immediate blame

ACTIONS

1. How often do your actions match your words? Always, mostly, sometimes?

2. How can you consistently ensure that you meet the commitments you make?

3. Do all people you interact with feel secure in the knowledge that you will deliver what you say you will? How do you know this?

4. Do you use your authority to create trust? How do you do this?

5. How have you created an atmosphere that openly encourages trust?

EMPOWER
acknowledge
recognize
truthful
shared-authority
parposeful
confidence delegate inspired

LIFE HABIT FIVE
Empower Others

*"There are two kinds of leaders–
those who are comfortable sharing their power
and those who want absolute control of it."*

Empowering others requires not only your full attention but also clarity, focus, and follow-through. The first four Life Habits place the focus primarily on you; in the case of empowering others, you must pay as much attention to others as you do to yourself.

Empowerment is a term that has been overused and is sometimes misunderstood. It has become a consulting buzzword, something to be said to create an atmosphere of trust and inspiration. But empowerment cannot be faked. You're either empowering others or you're not. There is no in-between.

Empowering others is a subtle yet distinct skill that brings out the best in those around you. When people feel empowered by their leaders, they seek to do more and better things because they want to. When you empower others, you are recognizing and acknowledging the best that people have to offer. When we feel empowered, we take more risks, work harder, and explore new things without the fear of being admonished for wasting time.

There are two simple ingredients for empowering others—sharing power and inspiration.

SHARING POWER

Sharing power might at first sound like a soft or simplistic step, but for many leaders it's about just letting go and no longer trying to do and control everything.

To effectively share power, you must be willing to let others make decisions and take actions on their own, allowing them to be responsible for getting things done. Leaders who are comfortable with empowerment are not afraid to surround themselves with people who are experts in areas where they are not. Delegation is a vital part of empowerment.

Leaders are sometimes fearful of losing their control or authority if they share power. They also fear being seen as weak. These types of leaders tend to rule by fear. To rule by fear is to destroy morale, innovation, and trust.

INSPIRATION

Seeking to inspire others might seem like a lofty objective, but it really isn't. To inspire is to simply set an example by always doing and being your best, regardless of the situation. When you are inspired, it is easier to naturally inspire others and evoke great results from those you lead.

The most powerful elements a leader has are his or her ability to influence or inspire others…to do more, to be more, to think bigger, to be more proactive, and to be the best that he or she can be. It sounds like a mouthful but it starts with you, the leader. A leader can purposefully nudge and guide employees in the direction of their goals. But leaders can only inspire others when they are inspired themselves.

EMPOWER OTHERS

To effectively empower others, you must be capable of comfortably sharing power and inspiring others. Empowerment requires conscious preparation. You not only need to expect people to succeed, you need to expect to be inspired.

The following self-assessment is a guide to help you gauge how well you understand and embrace the skill of empowering others.

INSTRUCTIONS: Read each statement. If the statement is true for you, check it.

____ I know the strengths and development needs of those I share power with (or empower).

____ I actively seek to be inspired on a daily basis.

____ I know I can effectively delegate and I have shown those I delegate to how to do the same.

____ Those I have empowered are not afraid to tell me the truth.

____ I walk my staff through simulated problems to give them practice and confidence in making decisions.

____ I select the right people for the right job—no one suffers in his or her position.

____ I surround myself with strong, talented people; I am not afraid to share my power with them.

____ I have identified a variety of people, places, and things that inspire me.

____ TOTAL

EMPOWERMENT

IS	IS NOT
Effectively delegating	Always taking control/ doing it yourself
Being understanding in difficult times	Intolerant and ready to pounce
Setting and keeping high personal standards	Rules are made for everyone but you
Praising others	Bragging
Seeking to be inspired	Never satisfied
The glass is full	The glass is never full enough
Delegating to the right people	Dumping duties on others
Providing clear expectations	Just do the best you can

Changing the world

ACTIONS

1. What could you begin doing tomorrow that would increase your opportunities to be inspired?

2. Who is the most inspiring person that you know?

3. Why does that person inspire you? In what ways could you be just as inspiring?

4. In what other ways could you seek to be inspired more frequently?

5. Who is the person who has inspired you the most in your life?

6. How can you as the leader/manager of your company or department make a bigger effort to show that you care?

action considerate
CHANGE energized
passionate
aware even-tempered
accountability
excited

ADDITIONAL LIFE HABITS
Awareness, Change, and Fear

> "I can accept failure,
> everyone fails at something.
> But I can't accept not trying."
> – Michael Jordan

YOUR AWARENESS LEVEL

Your ability to embrace the Life Habits will always be equal to your level of awareness.

Within us are the physical, emotional, and spiritual components that represent who we are and what makes us happy. Few of us really know or understand how these components work, and even fewer know how we became the way we are today. Awareness can fill the gaps.

Without practicing awareness, I personally would have missed fifty percent of what has happened to me and around me. I would have allowed myself to become preoccupied with the usual time-killing, mind-cluttering habits (television, Internet-surfing, etc.).

Awareness enhances your life; start paying a little more attention and see what you start noticing.

INTENTIONAL CHANGE

Sometimes a leader is tempted to take a shortcut when affecting change. As a result, he may attempt change through force of will. This rarely works for long. To force change is to create fear, and fear can never create long-term success. Shortcuts lead to sloppiness and disregard toward customers and the company.

A leader must come from a place of *caring*. Thoughts such as, "I care about how my employees feel," or "I care that my customer is in trouble," or "I care about my friends" doesn't mean that a leader is soft, easy, or foolish. It means she is grounded and clear about what she stands for as well as what is important to the company and its growth.

As a general rule, we all tend to resist change. (Some of us more than others.) We can anticipate change, prepare for it, deal with it, and even cause it, but there are two other choices we need to recognize and avoid. The first is *resisting change*. The second is *reacting negatively to change*.

ELIMINATING FEAR

Love is not a word you commonly hear in the workplace and certainly not with regard to business decisions. But it should be used.

Love is best represented in a company where the attributes of trust, caring, and respect are evident on a daily basis. But it is not blind love. It is love with the intention to help, support, and serve others as well as yourself.

A leader models love when she encourages others to grow in spirit, capability, and profit. Genuine love comes from the spirit and the desire to want the best for yourself and others.

AWARENESS, CHANGE, AND FEAR

Effective leadership requires a leader to be aware, to seek change, and to eliminate fear in the workplace. Your words, actions, and attitudes have a major effect on those you lead.

The following self-assessment is a guide to help you gauge how well you consider and understand the effect that awareness, change, and fear have on you and those you lead.

INSTRUCTIONS: Read each statement. If the statement is true for you, check it.

____ I am fully aware and considerate of other people's feelings without being overly self-conscious or hesitant about what I do or say.

____ I am consistently aware of my environment and how it can positively or negatively affect those I lead.

____ I lead change primarily by my actions and not exclusively through my words.

____ I seek feedback from the change agents as well as from those affected by the change to ensure balance and progress.

____ I consistently hold people accountable versus scolding or lecturing them.

_____ I never lose my temper or respond in anger with those I lead.

_____ I have clear goals and objectives for myself and for those I lead.

_____ I believe that people come to work intending to do their best.

_____ I have more than enough energy to get through a busy day.

_____ I am genuinely excited about what I am doing.

_____ TOTAL

ADDITIONAL LIFE HABITS
Decisiveness, Courage, and Gratefulness

"Reflect upon your present blessings of which every man has many not on your past misfortunes, of which all men have some."

– Charles Dickens,
A Christmas Carol and Other Christmas Writings

DECISIVENESS

Your decisiveness will ultimately define your legacy as a person and as a leader.

In a world that has become more calculating and cautious, a leader will stand out because of her or his decisiveness—and sometimes this means taking action. Other times it means taking no action at all.

People who work for an indecisive leader usually feel confused, frustrated, and uninspired, while decisiveness shows that a leader is clear about his intentions and where he wants to go. This both guides us and reassures us that a leader is really leading.

The downside to decisiveness is that you can still make a bad decision. We all do. So decisiveness also means that you are not afraid to deal with tough issues. And if a bad decision is made, you rectify it.

In both large and small organizations, it is not uncommon to see mid-level managers avoiding sensitive customer or employee issues for fear of making a wrong decision or because it may upset the status quo. Senior management may have sent a signal that said, "We don't want you to handle this. Leave it alone." A decisive leader encourages, if not demands, that issues get handled openly, fairly, and quickly.

COURAGE

The decisive leader does not shy away from situations or issues that may be controversial or emotional.

It takes courage to push things through when they are not popular, but it takes even more courage to remain patient despite the cries for immediate results. The great leader knows the correct path to choose.

Fortunately, there are many good companies and good individuals in charge of them, and the leaders of those companies have taught me a great deal about patience, strategy, vision, and doing the right things for the right reasons.

Leaders who stand up for the employee as an individual and who believe in the equation *Employee + Customer + Stockholder = Success* inspire people. That is no small accomplishment in today's "show me the money no matter what" business climate.

Find the courage to ask questions, to express what you really want, and to consistently take action.

GRATEFULNESS

Gratitude for what you have is a powerful way to show that you care as a leader.

Society has become entitlement crazy. People seem to expect things without doing anything. And when they get it, they typically don't appreciate it. Sometimes they recognize and enjoy what they've received, but typically they immediately go looking for the next "thing."

We have all caught ourselves looking for more or wanting more, only to eventually awaken to the reality that we already have a lot to begin with. Usually this reawakening happens after we've lost what matters. Then our appreciation grows.

Avoid learning the hard way. Start practicing being grateful throughout your day. Force yourself to stop and look around. Create a new habit by actively searching for things to appreciate.

DECISIVENESS, COURAGE, AND GRATEFULNESS

The more a leader strives to be decisive, courageous, and grateful, the more human he or she becomes. Though you won't always be decisive, courageous, or grateful, the more you aim for them as ideals, the more likely that they will positively affect your leadership.

The following self-assessment is a guide to help you gauge how well you consider and understand the effect decisiveness, courage, and gratefulness have on you and those you lead.

INSTRUCTIONS: Read each statement. If the statement is true for you, check it.

____ When making a decision, I consider all parties and how it may affect them.

____ I aim to make decisions that are timely and complete.

____ I don't avoid or put off making a decision because it's difficult or because it involves a sensitive issue.

____ I fully recognize that sometimes it takes courage to speak up.

____ I am past the point of seeking the favor of others; I am my own person.

_____ I am not afraid to do the right thing for the right reasons.

_____ I speak up when it's imperative that I do so, not because it's convenient or self-serving.

_____ I make time throughout my day to appreciate the people, things, and circumstances that surround me.

_____ I actively look for reasons to say thank you.

_____ I consider myself lucky to be who I am and to have what I have.

_____ TOTAL

ADDITIONAL LIFE HABITS
Creativity, Service, and Solitude

"The monotony and solitude of a quiet life stimulates the creative mind."

– Albert Einstein

CREATIVITY

Artists create. Leaders create. Employees create. We're all artists. It's in our nature to create new things, circumstances, and opportunities, as well as a vision of the future.

This capacity to create diminishes over time because we've convinced ourselves (or have been convinced) that we can't or shouldn't create any longer.

Every kid in the world creates; they imagine being astronauts, firemen, ballerinas, princesses, cowboys, or detectives. And every one of those imagined situations are very real to them.

That's kid's stuff, but the inventors of the technology and toys that fill our world are really kids at heart. Imagining new stuff is fun and challenging to them. The only difference between them and us is that they didn't stop imagining when they were told to. (*Get your head out of the clouds, stop daydreaming,* etc.).

Creativity is one of the greatest opportunities to bring new and better things into the world.

So create—that new project, that new customer service program, that new marketing approach, or that new building design.

SERVICE

One of the most powerful actions a leader can take has nothing to do with decisions, strategy, or vision; it's simply being of service to others. I'm not talking about serving coffee here. This is about proactively looking for ways to move people and circumstances forward through service to others.

When leaders serve, they ask, "How can I help?" They make requests, not demands. They know how to be naturally supportive, and they don't wait to be asked.

They know and believe that it's better to give and receive versus *Get – Get – Get.*

To serve others, whatever your role or position, is a powerful way to lead. It sends the combined messages of "I am giving," "I am caring," and "I have nothing to prove."

SOLITUDE

If you fill up your life with too many things—activities, obligations, to-do lists, overly demanding jobs, possessions, needs, and aspirations—chances are it will be very hard for you to see, much less think about *who* you are as a person...and as a leader.

Solitude leaves you open to possibilities.

Nearly every book on meditation urges us to find time and space to be alone, to still our thoughts, and to move away from the past and the future and be mindful of what is happening right in this instant.

Seeking solitude, or taking a *time-out* disengages you from a world filled with problems, biases, and judgments, and allows you space to just be. Solitude is an important component of self-care; don't skip it.

CREATIVITY, SERVICE, AND SOLITUDE

Making time and space to be alone allows leaders to regenerate their energy levels so they may be more readily available to serve others and give themselves the space to be creative.

The following self-assessment is a guide to help you gauge how well you consider and understand the effect that creativity, service, and solitude have on you and those you lead.

INSTRUCTIONS: Read each statement. If the statement is true for you, check it.

____ I actively look to create a vision for the future that benefits as many people as possible.

____ I enjoy the conscious activity of creating, without boundaries or judgment, so that new things are possible.

____ I encourage others to create.

____ I consider those around me to be creative artists, and I allow mistakes to occur without getting angry or upset.

____ I recognize that everyone needs quiet time—even me.

____ I make time during the day to disconnect from the world and still my mind.

____ I encourage others to take time out to think or to just be still.

____ I believe and live by the motto of consciously serving others.

____ I have fully learned how to give without expecting something in return.

____ I feel it is a privilege to serve others.

____ TOTAL

A NEW OPPORTUNITY
to Lead and Serve

The word habit may be a fairly overused term in self-help books, but there are very few words that you can use in its place.

There are similar words, like *custom* or *practice* or *tradition*, but *habit* seems to fit perfectly. The thing about habits is, if you practice them long enough they become who you are, and then there's no need to use the word anymore.

Who we are is more important than any label that can be applied to us. Who we are is defined by our actions, by our feelings, and by the results we create in our lives—such as a positive, motivated workplace, or a loving, happy family, or friendships that last a lifetime.

YOU DON'T HAVE TO BE HEROIC, JUST COURAGEOUS

Despite the numerous books on the subject of leadership, leadership can be simply defined as nothing more than *being an inspiration to other people*. Those who lead typically want to inspire others. Perhaps they, too, have been touched by their own leaders' words, actions, and vision.

You don't have to be a hero to be a leader, but real leadership does require courage. You must be willing to do the right things for the right reasons, despite what popular opinion espouses.

We have all worked with or worked for inspiring leaders, as well as for those who were less than honorable.

Uninspiring people who end up in leadership positions make decisions that are self-serving and often hurtful. These leaders have personal motives, such as fame, wealth, power, or recognition. These personal motives send a strong signal to employees and to the public that it's okay to behave this way.

Employees typically scrutinize their leaders because they want to feel that they can trust them. Employees want reassurance that their leaders want to help them as much as their customers.

By working through the eight self-assessments in this book, you are setting yourself on a path to improvement—not to make yourself better than others, but to be the best leader you can be.

Acknowledgements

Thanks to: Derek Sivers, Fr. Frank O'Loughlin, Bill Moss, Bono, His Holiness the Dalai Lama, Stephen Q. Shannon, Rick Seymour, William F. Buckley Jr., Bill Gates, Dr. Michael Axelrod, Seth Godin, Dr. Andreas Tzakis, Monta Burt, Miguel Ruiz, Debbie Weppler, RN, Stephen R. Convey, and the past presidents of the Rotary Club of West Palm Beach.

And, as always, thanks to Maura and Vanessa.

Serving others is:

- Making a sincere offer to help before the other person has to ask.

- Giving back to the community in the form of your time as well as your money.

- Visibly showing respect to others regardless of who they are or what they are asking.

- Continuously modeling everything noted in this book; not because you feel you have to but because you want to.

Most of us want to be more, to become more motivated and more inspired. As a leader, it's more about *who* you are and less about *what* you are.

Finally, consider the Life Habits as perspectives, a starting point or place of reference for you to grow from. Most of us want to get better at what we do, and as a leader it is a never-ending process.

So go ahead, set the example. Trust, serve, and share—others will follow.

Some leaders still teach and model the value of patience, strategy, vision, and doing the right things for the right reasons. Employees will look to see that their leader's actions match his words. This is a tremendous responsibility, and it provides real opportunity for a leader. The simple act of sharing a few words to inspire others, and reinforcing those words with action, is one of the most powerful attributes a leader can possess.

Most of us like to be inspired by others—in word and in deed. We seek leaders out. We are attracted to them. Though they may be total strangers, we feel a connection, an affinity that connects us to them in inexplicable ways. When you fully recognize that connection as a leader, you will begin to lead intentionally, knowing that you can have a positive impact on those around you.

One of the most inspiring actions we take as leaders is when we serve others. The concept of the servant leader is not a new one, but it's worth familiarizing ourselves with it. To be a servant leader is more than doing things for others; it's an attitude that incorporates empathy, awareness, and stewardship with hard work and the enjoyment of life.

Serving others goes way beyond the menial.

About the Author

Jeff Pasquale is an Executive and Life Coach who works specifically in the areas of life, leadership, and legacy. He has been coaching for 20 years.

He lives in Boynton Beach, Florida.

More information about Jeff can be found at www.JeffPasquale.com

He is the author of: *Airport Life: How to Relate at Any Altitude*, *The Book of Leader: A Testament to the Art of Leadership*, *The Magic Dance: Do You Lead, Follow, or Get Out of the Way?*, *How BIG is Your Target?: The Power of Focus in a Cluttered World*, *Looking for SUNSHINE: A Practical Guide for Dealing with Life's Challenges*, *Subway Life: An Underground Guide to Balanced Living*, *Get That Promotion: Manage Up and Get There Faster*, and *Get That New Job: Self-Coaching Steps That Work*.

NOTES

NOTES